Greyhound Diary

Lulu.com

An imprint of Lulu Publishers
c/o Lulu Enterprises, Inc.
3131 RDU Center, Suite 210
Morrisville, NC 27560

www.lulu.com

Copyright © James Inman 2005

James Inman asserts the moral right to be
identified as the author of this work.

Printed and bound by Lulu at www.lulu.com

All rights reserved. No part of this publication may be reproduced,
stored in a retrieval system, or transmitted, in any form or by any
means, electronic, mechanical, photocopying, recording or otherwise,
without the prior permission of the publishers.

This book is sold subject to the condition that it shall not, by way of
trade or otherwise, be lent, re-sold, hired out or otherwise circulated
without the publisher's prior consent in any form of binding or cover
other than that in which it is published and without a similar condition
including this condition being imposed on the subsequent purchaser.

To Scott Wisner, his wife and adopted son.

Greyhound Diary
A Travel Guide

JAMES INMAN

Introduction

At a card shop somewhere on the road, I found a blank book with Edvard Munch's *The Scream* on the front cover. I thought it would be entertaining to jot a few things down. I had to get to Portland and I wasn't looking forward to the trip. The first few entries were written on a Greyhound bus as I rode out the throes of acute alcoholic withdrawal. Most people would just describe it as a hangover, but a medical term provides a much more lucid description. My original idea was to put down some thoughts for the amusement of my friend Emery, much like Erasmus wrote *Praise of Folly* for Thomas More. It was somewhere around Omaha when I decided to document the entire journey. Initially this was not intended for public consumption and could easily be titled, *"A Secret Diary of Hate."* I have altered very few lines, resisting the simplistic urge to cut things that may offend or disturb. This is not a novel disguised as a diary; it's more like an exorcism. For those of you who have never taken a non-stop bus trip across America, I expect to be speaking to the little devil inside who says, "This is just too depressing not to laugh at."

1

I'm sitting in a coin operated TV chair with 15 channels of gray snow on the screen. The ceiling speaker is blasting horror sounds of "Sioux City! Sioux Falls! Fargo! Connecting final call through Gate 13! Final boarding call!" Along the wall a row of violent video games groan explosions of chaos, gunfire and electronic screaming. Stupid jerk-ass dick selling hot dogs and all I needed was a cup for some ice water and he said it was 95 cents unless I had a ticket, I show him the ticket and he throws the cup at me. The bathroom smelled like a steaming wall of vitamin-fortified piss. The speaker is spewing obscenities again: "Final boarding call for Sioux City, Sioux Falls, by way of Anchorage, Jacksonville, Los Angeles, Nova Scotia. You'll be zigzagging across the country arriving four days late, surrounded by nine tick-infested screaming kids! Final boarding call!"

I got my suitcase on with no problems. Nobody asked me if my bags had been in my possession the whole time or if I packed them myself like the airport. I could have a suitcase full of heroin, plastic explosives and human body parts. No one would care or notice.

"Please remain inside until bus departure is announced. Visitors not allowed on platform! And this is your third round of last and final boarding calls in a series of final boarding calls to Sioux City! Limping along at 10 mph, traveling in no particular direction! With occasional stops at smelly diners, truck stops and run-down terminals, then back on the no-good travel Shit Rod for non-stop boredom with freak-show white trash! Final boarding call!"

As I climb on the bus I'm reminded of *Dante's Inferno*. "Abandon all hope, ye who enter here."

Speaking of hope, I'm hoping some pig farmer doesn't try to sit next to me. I put my backpack in the empty space as a non-verbal clue to stay back and keep moving. As we roll out on the highway, it's another public address of "No smoking in the bathroom! No alcoholic beverages allowed on the bus! If you have headphones, make sure it's not as loud as my speaker system or I'll leave you on the side of the road! No masturbating in the aisle or rude behavior! Sit down, shut up, and don't stare at anybody!" The lady next to me has a sandwich and I want to grab and throw it at the driver's head. But he'll probably say, "No sandwich throwing and no pestering old women! Final boarding call!"

This is not a smooth ride. My hand is bouncing around the page. It's quiet now because we all know we're trapped like bunnies in the jaws of a Greyhound. Sandwich Lady just bent over and stuck her butt in my face to get a snot rag out of her suitcase.

We pass the first town at two miles an hour. This is not an actual road. I think we're driving across a field. The driver took a wrong turn and we're now on our way to Jonestown. There's a signpost up ahead: *Welcome to Impending Doom!* Occult Masonic Rotary signs bolted across the bottom. We must be collecting the Illuminati. Where the hell are we going?

Here's our first stop. The speaker system kicks in and the driver says we are not allowed in the grocery store because people have been left there so we get this nine-hour speech about not going in the grocery store because he'll leave us there. About 10 convicts from some work release program climb on board. A goddamn prisoner sits next to me. He looks like a cross between Madam Blavatsky and Charles Starkweather. The guy behind him is talking about the prison rules and why his cellmate needs to learn a few things about how to keep his mouth quiet.

Here's another stop the blind idiot driver made. Un-fucking-believable. Remember, people who ride the

Wounded Grey Squirrel are lower-class, migrant-worker poor, under-$700-a-year earning people. They bring their own food, but the bus does stop at times for people to eat. So, get this—the Brainless Monkey Driver stops at an *airport* for our dinner break so we have to buy airport food! *Expensive* airport food, like 20 bucks a sandwich! Nobody has money to buy anything. People are grabbing sugar packets and sharing hot dogs. And of course, it's an airport that doesn't sell alcohol. What are the chances we found the Joseph Smith Mormon International Idiot Fuck Airport? I buy half a candy bar for $15. What kind of scam is this? The driver must be getting some kickback from the pretzel court candy bar shack, or maybe he just thinks he's an actual airline pilot. We get five minutes here. Surveillance cameras are everywhere, so there's no way to steal anything. Some old ex-topless-dancer-turned-lunch-lady is slinging the crap and the only food item is a hot dog turning on a wheel heated by a light bulb. "Yes, I'll take that rotating, room-temperature meat dildo for nine dollars. And could you please kick me in the face and stomp on my neck with those white plastic cafeteria fuck-me pumps?"

Back on the bus, the driver doesn't even look back to see if everyone is on. He just jumps in and starts driving. Someone is running back from the bathroom with his pants halfway down. He stands in front of the bus like the guy in the Tiananmen Square tank standoff. There's a long moment of silent tension. The bus driver finally lets him on. We slump into our seats for another 12 hours of endless nothing. Nobody talks. We are all afraid.

I'm now crushed between two seats and my face is in this leech-infested tuft of purple gray hair. Why can't I get somebody with posture to sit in front of me? Instead it's all these *"I wanna be flat and sleep like on a hospital bed. No one is on the bus but me"* types. Hey! Stroke Lady! Can you back the seat off my cock? I'm inhaling cake crumbs from your 100th birthday. How did you get cake in the hair? Does that hairnet keep cranium bugs from eating the eyes out of your sockets? Did you buy your skull from a garage sale? How far back are you going to stretch out? I can't feel my legs. If my foot turns green and falls off from the bus parasites, I'm using my own detached limb to beat you on the side of your disabled head!

The indoor port-o-potty on this bus smells like heated urine boiling on a campfire fueled by human waste. Worst stink imaginable. The door's shut and it still seeps out. And blue water is not natural. A blue turd smells the same as a regular turd, it's just blue now, and I can't inhale. I spot a Styrofoam hamburger box swimming around the blue piss aquarium. I want to reach in, pull it out and show the driver. He'll stop the goddamn bus and we'll sit on the side of the highway till we get a confession: "Final boarding call! What is this Styrofoam hamburger box doing in the bathroom hole? Who eats food while they take a dump? This is a violation! Is there a turd inside of this? What in the Wide World of Sports is going on here, people?"

All buses are shaped like giant aluminum coffins, only larger, with windows. They use aluminum coffins for hauling dead soldiers and mass murder victims. If you ever had a load of dead people to bury all at once, you could use a bus. You could just drive it into a hole and bury it. No flowers, just empty potato chip bags to mark the spot.

Jim Jones used to ride the bus all the time. That's where he got the inspiration for mass suicide. He took a bus from Alaska to Florida and the idea just popped in his head. A kind, devoted minister before the trip, but after a few hundred miles he starts wearing dark sunglasses. "What's the use people? Let's take a bus to South America and end it all. I'll sell monkeys door to door and buy nine hundred bus tickets. Who's with me on this?" I bet the cyanide-spiked Kool-Aid was actually blue disinfectant water he pumped into a trash can from a discarded bus toilet.

Greyhound has an ad campaign with giant posters hanging from the ceiling of the most beautiful people. I've never seen anyone on a bus that looks like this. They're models from the Greyhound propaganda machine. It's like a catalog of pretty faces floating in the air, and we all stare up like they're gods hovering in the Greyhound Temple. There's never any scars or bumps on the head. If they had real pictures of real people who ride the bus, it would say *"Please give to your local charity"* or *"Alcoholism is a disease."* Maybe they string this up to give us hope. Shiny happy people you never see anywhere near a bus station.

On the back of each poster there's a slogan: "Be with the one you want to be with." You know what? I don't want to be with these people. I don't want to talk to these people. I don't want to sit next to these people. Where are the ad campaign people?

At the ticket counter I ask the customer rep, Latoya, if she ever had to ride the bus. Her head cocks back and she bursts out laughing. "No fucking way, you crazy white devil! I could print myself out a ticket to anywhere in the free world and I still won't ride that monkey-ass bus." This is not a good omen.

I hit the Greyhound Café, buy a pink lemonade and add a shot of my covert Travel Fuel. This bottle of cheap Russian Vodka has a label on the back that says, "Distilled in Jeff City, Missouri." What a complete rip-off. It's backing up my windpipe with that homeless-rolling-in-the-gutter alcohol smell. I overhear people talk about their bus breaking down 10 blocks from the terminal. Everybody had to walk. Bad vibe from the teenage girl with dreadlocks. She's headed to Canada with the look of fear. The terminal is now filling up with the tired, hungry and poor. Army duffel bags, hippie backpacks, aqua-green Samsonite makeup boxes. The cook is now shutting the chain wall and herding us out. "Let's go, people! Final boarding call!"

The only thing people read on the Joad Family Transporter is the Bible and books about serial murder. Half the people are praying out loud; the other half are laughing at some severed head joke. Sometimes a guy will just start mumbling, "I'm going to kill that shithead driver. I'll drive this goddamn bus straight through downtown Omaha. Fuck 'em! I'll paint a giant guitar on the side, like Ricky Skaggs." Actually when you hear "I'm going to kill that shithead driver," it doesn't sound that wrong. And no one will ever get arrested, like on a plane. Everybody mumbles this, even the Amish Lady. I bet she's churning out elaborate poems right now on her embroidered pillows: *"God please grant me the serenity to stab the driver in the head with an ice pick, and please let me suck out the brain water for refreshment."* The driver has no brain—just spinal fluid. Maybe she'll jam a long rubber tube in his ear so we can drink something. Those Amish have spunk and a quick sense of murder. On the farm, they do all their own slaughtering. They never waste a thing. And what's a little human flesh? We may have to go that route if we don't stop for food soon. Calm, determined survival. After a non-stop bus trip a guy could take a chunk out of his own arm.

2

I'm in a half-awake, zombie-like state. Time creeps by slow motion on the Freak Roller. It's now 6:30 a.m. again and I'm too tired to be pissed. Our driver has a speech impediment. When he gets on the PA, you need some sort of secret decoder ring to decipher the unintelligible crap. "O tay peotal twis hiss stape wouis an twe arw topping heare so u tan geet dah fak bakon and gech one you ne boss." Everyone looks up and tilts their head to the *"What the hell was that?"* angle. Total gibberish. I thought we're in another part of the world. Might as well be listening to white noise.

The guy next to me has all his crap in a white plastic bag. His head is down as he nods off in junkie dream time. Looks like there's a hickey or bite mark on his arm.

At the terminal somebody just informed the security guard about a rolled up plastic diaper on the floor. The wannabe cop picked it up, looked it over, and then tossed it back on the floor. Throw it in the trash fuckhole. What else do you have to do? You're guarding nothing but crippled old people. The only guy who can do any real damage is asleep. The shit filled diaper is still sitting there. The custodian walked by and swept up around it.

I snap a quick picture of a homeless man with a half-gallon of milk and a 40-ounce of Old Milwaukee he pulls from a plastic sack and sets on the ticket counter. Nobody says a word to this guy. There's no drinking allowed on the bus or in the bus terminal and he's mixing milk with beer right in front of the security guard.

Meet some of the passengers:

The Stinky Priest sits next to you and you think it's going to be OK, because he's a man of the cloth, but then you find out the cloth hasn't been washed since John the Baptist lost his head. When's the last time you were baptized, Father? Could you please sprinkle holy water over your entire body and mix some soap with it? If cleanliness is next to Godliness, this man is pure evil. He needs a full immersion while the entire congregation prays for a Speed Stick. I'm praying for a slight breeze to blow the scent the other way. But it's all in vain. Somebody else would have to deal with the curse, and lose all faith in God and the Devil. Sweet Mother of Christ, please come and cleanse this man; he's possessed. I know when the devil is present because of the smell of sulfur, but this is worse than sulfur. This is like a spoiled bat wing. This is Baphomet's running shoe. Maybe he just got back from an exorcism and the possessed girl shot green puke on his shirt, but he didn't have time to wash it off. I think I'll go to the bathroom to get away from the stink. I can breathe much easier in there. God has granted the gift of smell but I now know it to be the fall of man.

The Sleepy Crackhead always gets the back three seats, and he always wants to know if the bus stopped in the last town and if he slept through it. Why do you ask me this, you deaf pimp? The bus driver can wake a dead man with his microphone of war. It's like a trumpet from Revelations. And why does the Crackhead get the back three bed-like seats? Because he's the one, the *only* one who can ignore the stench of the blue turd and sleep through the smell. And who can sleep on this Dog Machine? Fucking Rip Van Winkle? No! It's Sleepy Crackhead with his red Einstein hair and his bell-bottom jeans. Not hip, retro bell-bottom jeans, just the same jeans he never took off since 1978. He's got a Bad Company T-shirt with mustard stains from the giant pretzel he bought in Reno. The supposed-to-be-piping-hot-but-never-are Super Pretzels, with chunks of salt he picks off and stares at like a hit of crack.

Work Release Prisoners: They wear plain gray pants and gray shirts and look somewhat well adjusted except for the homemade tattoos on their neck that say "KILL" or "SATAN." This group has the best stories because they're always jabbering away about cutting off someone's head, or the protocols of anal sex and the hierarchy of who gets it and why, and if they catch the guard with his back turned they'll wrap a tube sock around his neck. Why Greyhound transports prisoners is beyond me. One guy is staring into the back of the seat as he burns in his gang monogram with a lighter. The smell of the charred seat cushion has now merged with the blue diesel fumes. The idiot driver is oblivious. The only difference between a driver and a Work Release Prisoner is the shiny Greyhound nametag. Everything is gray on the bus. The seats, the walls, even the floor. A Work Release could be operating this Prison Lift for all we know. All you need is a nametag. How can you tell the difference? They're like the driver's doppelganger. Even when we take a wrong turn, it's hard to tell if it's a real driver or not because bus drivers take wrong turns all the time. The only thing you can do is grab the PA microphone and scream "LOCK DOWN!" If it's a real driver, he'll just look at you like you're a dumbass.

Every time we stop there's the Old Man somewhere up front blocking the aisle. This guy walks like nobody's behind him, at one-tenth normal human speed. He's like an ice shelf, moving across the globe. Wherever we go, we're halfway there. When we stop, it takes the same exact amount of time to get off the bus as it did to get there. I'm getting paranoid thinking this guy was just like me when he got on the bus, but he got stuck in line behind another old guy who wouldn't get off or out of the way or move an inch. Maybe he's a reptile with a rotted brain and he thinks its cold outside, so he's hibernating while he's walking. He's a dead man walking, like a guy walking to an electric chair without the aid of the executioner pushing him along. We're waiting to move a fucking millimeter. I'm getting old just standing here. And it doesn't matter if you scream at his head. He can't hear, he can't even move. It's like *Dawn of the Dead*, or watching a turtle documentary in slow motion. I want to push him back down in his seat every time he gets up in front of me. Sorry, Mr. Father Time, I've got to get off here before the sun explodes.

Back on the Hound some fat woman came by to use the bathroom and she had a giant blood or shit stain on her ass. It had to be one of the grossest most weird things I've ever seen. She can't even fit into the bathroom. I look over and all I see is this fat ass with thin light blue work out pants and a long reddish-brown stain. I want to kick her ass to help her get inside but I don't want that crap on my shoe. I turn my head in denial, and get another full view from the reflection off the window. It's some stain like a slit artery or bad miscarriage. Did she botch her own self-abortion? She kept going in and out of the bathroom, and I swear she was hiding a coat hanger somewhere. Hey Bloodshit Lady, I'll give you $300 to get the job done professionally. Just get your blood-soaked ass out of my face!

2:00 a.m. Stopped somewhere and bought a piece of chicken. Sandwich Lady is sucking on a boiled egg.

I get ejected from the bus because of some mistake with the boarding call. Now I have to wait for the next bus. At least I'm clear of the Bloodshit Lady. Her seat area smelled like puke when I walked by. Someone must have shot the mouth stream.

Six hours to wait and no Grey Café. When I get to the next terminal, I'll look for a hotel, kill myself and then get back on the bus.

I collapse in the terminal to a vivid, half-awake dream. The driver is dressed as a clown. He pulls the bus over, and we all step into a bar. There's free beer, Black Flag on the jukebox and tattooed naked girls casually walking around. The mind takes care of itself on long bus trips. It's nature's way of saying everything is OK and none of this is really happening to you.

3

There's a McDonald's a block away, so I head over for a cup of coffee. The girl behind the counter has the smallest head on the biggest body I've ever seen. Her brain box looked like a spinal cord with eyes, connected to the torso of a giant sea cow. Some guy is dragging around a mountain bike with no wheels. He brought it into McDonald's and dumped it in the middle of the floor. The tiny-head woman tells him to move it or get the hell out. She reminds me of that baby-headed creature growing out of the guy's stomach in the movie *Total Recall*. It's the same head but her body is like Mike Ditka's. I try to use the bathroom, and of course I have to buy some food first to get a token for the pay-toilet to take a dump. McDonald's? Billions served? You know how many times I've eaten at McDonald's? I think they owe me a couple of free trips to the bathroom. Next time I find a locked bathroom at McDonald's, I'm going to jam a turd into the vent on the hand dryer and fill the entire place up with heated shit-air.

Back at the station, I spot a guy sitting behind a desk with a sign that clearly states, "Travel Aid & Tourist Information." I ask him when our bus departs and he says, "I don't know. I'm just sitting here." You fuck! So *I'm* the dumb ass? Why the hell are you sitting there? I watch 50 people walk up to this nutsack, ask information and he still wouldn't move. On the wall, I spot his picture. Employee of the Month.

The P.A. is on again. It's a very loud piercing scream like a jet engine in the ceiling. This sound can produce open sores on top of your head. It's always garbled and somebody could be chanting demonic praise to Satan but no one would know because it all goes in the subconscious. It's like a Motörhead concert in here with pure distortion vibrating the ceiling tiles. Chunks of asbestos are falling all around me. Every time they turn on the PA it starts the feedback. It's like a podium microphone without the podium just the metal adjustable foot long mic stand like a short robot's spine. When they move it around there's a wrenching sound, metal scraping metal, feedback and then the devil voice. I feel as if someone put a leaf blower next to my ear. You can't make out anything. It's like the whole place is on fire and whoever is speaking is being burnt alive. That's close to the same tone.

I got screwed out of a seat somehow. The punk baggage handler said I had to wait till 9:30, so like a blind sea bat I climb off and hang around the station. After about an hour, I realize I got the Greyhound-shaft re-route. I found a real information specialist and he clued me in on the scam. So I catch the next bus and it was worth the delay. I sit up front with the driver and tell him how I asked a baggage handler for information. He's all laughing teeth and wild eyes. He says they do that sometimes to punish passengers on a purely random basis—could have been a wannabe driver, or a junkie with a stolen Greyhound jacket. Who knows? It's five a.m. and my thinking is blurred. After asking nine people wearing official-looking Greyhound T-shirts, I was glad to finally find a man with experience. It's very spooky getting dumped off at the wrong location.

I'm having another series of half-awake, half-dream states and the inside of the bus is like a Francis Bacon painting. Too much coffee and vodka. My neck is bent in a wrong direction and the spinal cramp is producing hallucinations. The back of someone's head turns into a chicken wing or a rat face with tentacles and guns, like a William S. Burroughs nightmare.

The Talking Lady talks non-stop, like a perpetual mouth machine. Could be about her panty hose; could be about the weather. It doesn't matter what it's about, it's just all about her and her jabbering pie-hole. It starts to sound like a beeping noise, and after a while you forget she's talking. You just notice this constant sound in the background. Like a water wheel with ignorant noise grating on the ears. Then you realize she's still talking and it's not some sound the engine is making. I want to walk right up to her and scream in her face,

"Would you please SHUT THE FUCK UP! You stupid old whore, you could talk through a blowjob!" Oh, God, it's on and on and on about nothing, just like a talking metronome. You could set an atomic clock by the movements of her jaw and her fake fucking teeth. She probably goes through three pair a week grinding down the ivory. Maybe I'll lodge a Snapple bottle inside her throat or crush her larynx with my suitcase. "Oh, I'm sorry, I seemed to have smashed your skull with my backpack filled with rocks. Does anyone have a sock filled with shit to plug this hole? It's still going."

Old Black Sleeping Lady is the only person who can sleep on the bus besides the Crackhead in the back. Why? Because she lives on the Greyhound. All her stuff is in a paper sack and you want to wake her up from the coma and ask her the secret. How can she doze off and not move for 10 hours? I think she's dead and nobody cares. She's got her ticket crumpled up in her fist. We're way passed her stop and the driver lets her ride. He doesn't want to wake her because they film this scene for Greyhound commercials to show everyone it's possible to sleep on a bus. Leave the Driving to Us! And look! People sleep like rocks. It's a sleep mobile. It's like Demerol and chamomile tea; chloroform and melatonin. It's vodka, Phenobarbital and chocolate pudding spiked with decaffeinated Nytol. Hey, if she can do it, everyone else can. Right? Just move the seat back a half-inch and curl up like a hamster. Don't worry about making noise. A shot of human adrenaline in the heart couldn't wake Old Black Sleeping Lady. The entire bus could be on fire and a rescue team could pull her out with the Jaws of Life and dump her on the head and she still wouldn't wake up from that peaceful

slumber. She's dreaming of Barry White at the Waldorf
Astoria, drinking champagne and listening to the sounds
of Motown with Martin Luther King preaching "I have
a dream: Rosa Parks will sleep wherever the hell she
wants." Please, just tell me how the fuck you do this!

The Battered Wife is traveling to Oklahoma City, along
with her special-needs child chanting, "Mommy, when
will we be there? Mommy, are we there yet? Mommy,
will we be there soon? Mommy, can I grow up to be
like the work-release man? Is he my daddy? Did you
fuck Mr. Starkweather in the port-a-turd? Because our
foreheads look the same. They have the same shape,
like the evolution pictures they show me in science
class like a mirror. Mommy, can I get a prison tattoo?
Mommy! Mommy! Mommy! Mommy! Mommy!
Mommy!" My God, it's like a grown-up version of the
Eraserhead baby. And while we're on the subject, this
entire trip is a lot like a David Lynch movie marathon.
The group consciousness has the flavor of an angry
mob looking for a rope with no Negro to hang. They
have the will and the same gut rage, but we all know if
anyone is going to die, it should be the driver. Someone
should chuck a vodka bottle upside his head. Maybe I'll
tell the Starkweather boy we're at baseball camp.
"That's it, Corey. You'll be the next Jim Palmer some
day. You know him from the commercials, he works at
The Money Store. Throw this at the driver's head and I
promise to stop Mommy before she beats you to certain
death." She's asleep now anyway, or at least acting like
it each time her boyfriend screams, "Move your
goddamn legs, you retarded bitch!"

Rainbow Girl is the hippie chick with dreadlocks and armpit hair. She's always reaching for a water bottle, so everyone can get a glimpse of the growing-forest armpit shot: "Hey, look at me! I'm natural granola-crunching wood nymph spinning out in wandering monkey world!" Ever see that Saturday morning kid's show *Land of the Lost*? I think she played Cha-Ka's love interest. Cha-Ka had a drinking problem and used to beat her so she hit the road searching for Jerry Garcia. She never looks at anybody and no one looks at her. She just glides by in a force field of patchouli, "I'm the earth mother, but I'm riding the bus to Branson, Missouri!" If she falls asleep with her arms behind her head I'm going to squirt Nair on her pits and she'll melt like the Wicked Witch of the West. Her dreadlocks will be the only thing left on the seat. They'll smolder and spark and send out an odor of dead grapes, burning fire ants and ten-year-old candle wax. You could use the charred hair pile for space shuttle tiles because they can withstand heat up to 13,000 degrees Fahrenheit. What the hell happened, Rainbow Girl? Did you wash your hair with motor oil and Super Glue? How'd you train your armpits like Buckwheat's head? Cha-Ka still loves you but he's in prison now.

4

I find it nearly impossible to sleep on the bus. I've got two seats to myself and I'm in the fetal position with my legs stretched across the aisle and my feet on the opposite arm rest. I cramp up after five minutes, so I switch to the inverted fetal position with my legs under the seat and my head in the aisle. This lasted one whole second, until I got a kink in the neck. So I switch back to where I was originally. I'm struggling for a while not getting that certain groove when I realize I've been kicking this lady right in the head! I don't know how long this went on, but I do know it was at the very least five or 10 hard jams with the foot. At one time I may have even rested my feet directly on her head and she never moved. She must have been in some kind of deep Greyhound REM sleep. After three days, your body will just collapse. The Chevy truck commercial comes to mind, *"Like a Rock."* That old Bob Seger tune, like a fucking rock with kicks to the head asleep, dead asleep, drooling-naked-heroin sleep. Then I'm thinking maybe

I conked her out. That's got to be a weird shift of consciousness. Woken up with a foot to the head, only to be knocked back out again with the next blow. Dreaming of bricks coming down then everything goes black. Horrible nightmare swoon.

When I get off at the next terminal, the first thing I see is two Jehovah's Witnesses handing out the *Awake* magazine. How appropriate. I haven't slept all night. Where's the pamphlet *Deep Sleep?* Their God must be punishing me. And by the way, I've read the Bible and there's not one parable on the extended bus trip. All the cartoons in this pamphlet show people smiling and happy. What a cruel thing to pass out at a bus station. Those happy witnesses don't have to climb back on. I'd like to see how long their faith holds out on this shit train.

Sleep deprivation is producing horrible visions and paranoid confusion. I'm in the bathroom at the station and my urine stream is in a Z pattern. My eyes are unable to focus. I could be at the trash can, I can't really tell. Not sure which person I can trust for information. The public address system is pulsing out colors and lightning bolts of garbled sound. I think I see some toothless old man gumming a pizza, but it could be a toothbrush or pet snake. My hands feel like webbed feet. I'm seeing rabid greyhound dogs everywhere, foaming vicious grinning skinny hounds of hell chasing my brain and digging into the back of my neck for a chunk of bone meat. Greyhounds are known to suck marrow directly out of the spine. Howling wolf teeth dripping shiny fluid, like the movie *Alien Resurrection* with the fat Bloodshit Lady as Sigourney Weaver. And here she comes again. You goddamn evil troll. I'll give you my pants and walk around in my fucking underwear if you just quit bending over in my face.

This looks like a new bus. Not too crowded; one person for every couple seats. No ugly smell yet. This could be a trick. Everything could go wrong. Grey Death-Hound No. 5017 is officially in motion. PA briefing with the same speech on bus rules and regulations, but no announced time of arrival. Driver's name is Percy. Nice guy, but he's got a strange bump on his forehead.

This kid next to me is pulling a plastic bag over his head. His mom's asleep and I'm not going to get involved. He's climbing on the luggage rack. He's rolling on the floor, standing on his head, jumping around, climbing over the seats. He stares at me constantly. This kid is a non-stop sound machine. I'm getting very annoyed. I should ask him to put the bag back over his head. I'll tell him it makes him look like Batman with it on.

There's a way to take the armrest off and make a weapon. I've seen it done before. Next time the slobbering child gets wound up you can pop it off and smack him in the temple. It's made of soft plastic so it won't leave a mark. The temple is the best place to aim because it's the soft part of the head; this will stun the boy until he forgets what happened. The Battered Mom won't mind because she was probably going to do the same thing with a hidden vodka bottle. But don't try getting to know her or sit anywhere near. She's too damaged and may flinch each time you move your arm. Also two people beating on a child is not good, too much paperwork.

These goddamn Amish love their peanuts. I'm sitting across from a paranoid, little-house-on-the-prairie-girl in black. She looks like a chubby gargoyle chomping down on gravel, with her two hundred pounds of barn-raising flesh clutching that can like it's a post-apocalyptic food scrap. Every place we stop, it's the Gothic Marilyn Manson farmers with beards, peanuts, black clothes, mystifying hats like black flying saucers on their heads. Prairie Girl's husband looks sixteen, and already he's got the full beard. What's the secret? Must be all the backed-up semen. Every time I see the Amish, they're eating fucking peanuts.

Miles and miles of free entertainment, and my back is twisted in four different directions.

They just figured out that the destination town on the front of the bus is wrong. This has caused confusion at every terminal. They're fixing it now. I accidentally walk onto the wrong bus, and this security guard starts screaming in the most hillbilly fucked-up accent. I need a Toothless-Country-to-English dictionary. Somehow, I gather, this has become an international incident. He's waving his arms and jabbering. I'm like: "OK, Mr. Hatfield! Chill out! It's just a bus. It's not like we're on an airport runway or anything." I don't know if he understood; I should have added a twang sound or pulled out a few teeth. The bus still has the wrong destination on the front. I guess we'll have to wait until we get to a civilized town with mechanics who have opposable thumbs.

On the Jim Jones Retard U-Hauler #6027. Right behind the driver's seat is a bulletproof Plexiglas shield. To hit the driver in the head with a projectile, you have to lob it over and bounce it off the visor. What I really need is a propane tank—a big steel container of propane gas and a match.

Next terminal: I just stepped onto the set of *Coal Miners Daughter*. Conway Twitty and George Jones pictures all over the place, bolted-down banjos and guitars on the wall, no fast food nearby, no time to look around. I get some food at the Grey Café. turnip greens and a roll for $1.23. There's a kid with a bicycle helmet rolling on the floor and his mother is beating him with an aerosol can. The gift shop is filled with American flags and religious supplies, Johnny Cash coffee cups and Barbie doll purses. There's an old black man mumbling "Kill Whitey" and it's starting to make a whole lot of sense. I'll pull a banjo off the wall and start a race riot.

5

Grey Hound-Dog with Broken Head on Wheels. We just got through driving around in circles outside West Memphis. The driver couldn't find the stop. This guy is a complete incompetent. He's also a slow incompetent. We are now going 10 mph. We passed the same trailer three times. You cannot know the sheer horror. I am unable to explain myself right now from the angry disbelief. I may have to come back to this later.

Who let Amelia Earhart's retard brother at the controls? We're lost again! Even the kid with rickets is wondering out loud where the hell we're going. Where are the goddamn comment cards? I want a stack of five hundred to pass out to every passenger and their extended families. *Where are we?* He must be driving by sense of smell. That's why we're going in circles. He's chasing our own toilet breeze. Out in the middle of nowhere, crawling around at 10 mph like a headless fucking diseased turtle. If there ever was a driver who needed a vodka bottle upside the head, it's this guy. We had to actually pull over and ask for directions. I've never seen anything so funny in my life: a Greyhound bus driver, stepping out of a bus, in full Greyhound uniform, asking a group of people where the Greyhound bus stop is. We finally find it after an hour. Drop one person off. Roll back onto the highway at 10 mph. Incredible.

How can a bus driver get lost? What the hell kind of brain-damaged, vegetable-head of dead lettuce puts on a Greyhound name tag without knowing how to find his way back to the next station? Do they pass out uniforms to anyone who can scrawl their name on an application? A sleep-deprived rat can find a piece of cheese in a maze. A displaced cat can find its way home from four thousand miles away. Even a blind pigeon can circumnavigate the globe without asking directions. This is supposed to be an adult human being with a three-pound brain, but we're spinning in circles like a battery-powered toy. It's a rotating meaningless mural of pawn shops and empty Quik Stores like the background in a Flintstones cartoon with the lampshade and couch spinning past.

Greyhound fever dream, or note to self? Stab driver with pen in neck until dead. Dump body in crumpled mass on the stairs by the door. Take control of the wheel and PA system. Order every passenger to strip naked and toss all clothes out emergency exit. Stop at liquor store, stock up on Old Milwaukee. Duct-tape all children to the luggage rack. Connect iPod to sound system. Maintain cruising speed—100 mph on a direct path to the next stop.

We're still lost. Here's a list of slang terms for Greyhound: Misplaced Rolling Shit Coffin, Vanished Aluminum Death Box, Grey Death Hound, Kidnapped Turd Mobile, Vehicle for Shit Stains and Blood Women, Joad Family Transporter, Blood Bus, Puke Machine, Lost Rolling Puke Machine, No Good Travel Shit-Rod, Nowhere Anti-Bus, Wounded Grey Squirrel, Missing Child Retard Van, Negative Entropy Car, Aluminum Homunculus, Grey Aluminum Piss Container on Wheels, Wheels of Piss, Giant Rolling Box of Sleepless Bodies, Cheap Ass Travel Dog, Jonestown Dog-O-Death, Scrotum Roller, Scrotum Tow, Cage with Wheels, Turd and Puke Roll Machine, Freak Roller, Freak Hauler, Blind Man's Jet Ride, Devil Car, Demon Bus, Junkie Car, Prison Lift, Metal Mobile Crap House, Punk Ass Nowhere Cart Filled with Rotted Meat, Worthless Can Filled with Bile on Axles Made of Broken Spinal Columns from Captured Yeti Monsters, Nightmare Transportation for Retarded Homeless Psychopaths Eating Styrofoam Boxed Turds.

We arrive four and a half hours late. The driver runs off the bus with no announcement or apology. I try to complain at the ticket counter. She gives me the 1-800 customer service number. I call and it's a machine: "Due to an overwhelming number of calls, we are unable to accept your complaint at this time." No shit! Sounds like the phone lines are lighting up.

The gift shop is stocked with Greyhound merchandise everywhere. Greyhound toy miniature bus, Greyhound four-piece metal coaster set, Greyhound coffee cups, Greyhound collectable shot glasses, official Greyhound commemorative plates, Greyhound five-day deodorant pads, Greyhound condoms, Greyhound thermos... Ah yeah, I'd like a memento; maybe something to remember HOW WE WERE LOST FOR FOUR AND A HALF HOURS! How about a souvenir map for the driver? Got one of those?

The hairy-chest man with a giant gold crucifix hanging from his neck asked the cook at the Grey café for a knife to open his can of Spam because he broke off the pull tab. She gives him this foot-long kitchen knife and he spends most of the next hour hacking away at the can. The crucifix is bouncing off his hairy cro-mag chest. I don't know which is longer, the knife or the cross. He's wearing a yellow plastic fedora hat with Hawaiian shirt fabric wrapped around the brim. It's all very sublime. Jesus loves you man.

Next to me are two Catholics from New York talking to a blond German backpacker about concentration camps. It's all about genealogy, ethnic cleansing, Strasbourg and *their* people. Why don't they start a rally? It's fucking weird! They're talking heritage, Blood Purge, and Nazis war crimes. Priests cast into gas chambers, Protestant-Catholic split, Fatima, Medjugorje, Mother Mary, very weird conversation. Now they're praying together. Catholic New Yorkers trying to convert a German Lutheran girl.

When we get to the next town for our break, everybody gets out—but as soon as they hit the parking lot; they make that long, groaning sound people make when they smell a dead body. We run into the truck stop for shelter and see pine-tree cardboard air fresheners on sale everywhere. The smell is like a dead truck driver floating bloated inside a sour milk tanker, with the curdled milk spilling out onto a hot plate and a fan blowing the disgusting fog right into your face. Even the people who smoke can't stand it; they just wait on the bus, afraid to go out. The bus is just a few feet from the truck-stop door, and people are running inside like it's raining shit. It was as if someone dumped goat vomit on the Stinky Priest and he sat in the sun for three days. What could it be? I ask the clerk; she becomes a bit withdrawn. Like it was something they had to endure but never spoke of. We're supposed to take a 15 minute break, but the driver just walks out with his hand over his mouth and jumps on the bus. He slams the door and stomps on the accelerator. We plunge back into the darkness.

6

A distorted PA briefing comes on: "Now boarding Fellini Boxcar Filled with Freaks, Gate 13. Stops at Dixon Junction, Jackson, Brownsville. No smoking, no intoxicants, no transfer or use of illegal drugs." This is going to be a hard ride. I feel a puke coming on. My nerves are on fire and I feel like I'm floating down some polluted river. My spinal column has a bad kink and my eyes are like rocks. I must have been a serial killer in a past life and I am now being punished. You cannot imagine the despair.

This driver's Plexiglas shield is lowered and his head is now vulnerable. Straight shot with a vodka bottle if he makes a wrong turn.

We are still parked at the station, waiting to leave. A refrigerator-sized black lady sits next to me and I swear I was pressed up against the window. There is no way we could sit like that. Her butt was a colossal bean-bag chair; a hulking, gelatinous mass. I finally get up and sit next to a normal-sized guy. She calls over her exploded sister. I have no idea how they wedged in there. This bus is full and nobody has a seat to himself. Some guy is making a ham sandwich next to me with a kid on his lap. We are now rolling; it's 10 p.m. This is where the ride gets tough. Kids screaming, everybody crunched in, dark inside. The people behind me are talking non-stop about the weather, Yellowstone National Park and why Uncle Tom is an alcoholic. Yap! Yap! Yap! I can't read. They're jabbering like long-lost friends. They just met and they're covering everything. Why don't you pull out the *World Almanac* and review every subject known to man in alphabetical order? Abraham, action movies, Amtrak, aneurysms, Atlanta, Aztec, basketball, beavers, Belgrade, bromide, blah fucking blah, Cameras, cake, corn, corn pads, crab cakes. On and on and on…

This particular driver likes his bus at a sub-freezing temperature. I had no idea it could get this cold. The vent is blasting arctic air right next to the window so I jam a newspaper down the hole to cut off the flow. Everybody has coats and blankets on. I asked the driver to turn the air conditioner down and it just got colder. It's like a refrigerator truck in here. I'm looking for something to start a fire with. I should get to my suitcase. Maybe I have some battery-powered socks to wrap around my head.

In a terminal bathroom. This old man has his shirt off and his pants down to his ankles, fully naked in the middle of the bathroom. Not inside a stall. Bent over, dick and nutsack hanging down, washing his ass with a T-shirt. Maybe I should tell the security guard. I hope he's not some ass-wiping exhibitionist. Have I just been the victim of a sex crime?

When we pull out, the drivers always honk a couple times. Children? Dogs? Just honk the horn. The good news: this new bus doesn't smell like piss. The bad news: I left my luggage on the bus that smells like piss. I forgot to get my suitcase from the overhead bin. I hope somebody finds it and puts it on the right bus. But it'll probably end up in West Memphis.

I've got another Energizer child next to me. He's been gumming the same McDonald's biscuit for the past two hundred miles. It's a soggy mass of drool and pasty-white dough crumbs. I might have to elbow this kid in the forehead. He's singing! "Jesus loves the little children." I hope he's ready to meet Jesus. Now it's "Bingo was his name-O." I need a small vial of elephant tranquilizer and a syringe with a needle that can penetrate the skull.

We stop for refueling. We get dumped off at this restaurant called the Lone Steer. On the wall they have these cozy little knick-knacks. Crutches! Who hangs crutches on the wall for decoration? Not the kind of thing you want to look at while you're eating. "Yes, can

I get that waitress with scoliosis and a Depends undergarment to wipe off my table?"

This trip is just getting too weird. A new passenger climbs aboard and says she overheard a woman at the last stop talking about a guy who shot himself on the bus. Incredible. Greyhound is a perpetual source of human tragedy. Suicide? We've all thought of it, but on the bus nobody has the means. If I had a gun, I'd pawn it and buy a plane ticket.

Undercover police bring a drug-sniffing dog out to check our luggage. They're going through everything. The narcotics officers look mean and determined. When we pull up, I sense something is about happen, because the driver ran off the bus and locked the door. Two unmarked cars pull up. Luggage is tossed out and the dog is now humping our bags. Everybody gets out of their seat to look out the window. The bus almost tipped over with all the weight to one side. We're looking at each other suspiciously. Who could it be? It's got to be someone on the bus. One guy has prison tattoos; people clear out of his way. He gets this dumb expression: "Hey, it's not me!" The undercover police are dressed like average bus passengers, except they're clean-shaven with perfect teeth. They're boarding the bus now, so we all scatter back. That's when I remember the half-empty vodka bottle in my backpack. I hope it's not an alcohol-sniffing dog. I look straight ahead and the dog comes up and sniffs my hand. I try to pet it but the undercover cop says, "Don't pet the dog, sir!" They keep looking. Nothing seems to really excite the dog. It whines a little when it sniffs the bathroom door. The cops get off the bus looking somewhat pissed.

One of the hardest things to do on a bus is turn your watch backward one hour when you cross a time zone.

There's Schizophrenic Tattoo Guy talking to himself about how we're all going to die in a nuclear holocaust. But he has to yell to understand himself, because he was born with no sense of other people. He's screaming: "We're all going to die! We're all going to burn in a nuclear holocaust!" Thank you, Mr. Illustrated Fuck-up. I was just sitting here, wondering if this trip could get any more depressing. Now I know it can, with you here. Wait! Come to think of it, worldwide nuclear extinction doesn't sound all that bad. Maybe a plague of locusts can be a good thing. If my body were to be ripped apart by Bible-sized insects, I wouldn't have to listen to your painted ass. And if you mark your body with permanent ink, please plunk down some real cash. Don't pay with cigarettes for the homemade jail art. There he goes again: "Everyone is going to die in a nuclear holocaust!" Is that how he picks up chicks, with his Dr. Doom routine? Is this from the appendix of a Dale Carnegie course on How to Win Friends and Influence People After You've Tried Everything Else? And, no, we are not all going to die in a nuclear holocaust. They can arm Global Hawk with laser-guided bombs to burn your ass specifically. And after you're gone, as it is written in the Book of Revelation, we shall rest peacefully for a thousand years.

Detox Woman just got out of jail and jumped the bus to Eugene for a state-sponsored dry out. She has seen it all, shooting heroin for 22 years, and this is her last chance. Someone is waiting in an unmarked van to take her directly to a clinic. Every time we stop she contemplates making a run for it, but she knows she won't get far because she can't stand up too long without collapsing. She tells me all about prostitution and rape. Trading a blowjob for a 40-ounce. At least this woman is somewhat interesting. She has more than a few stories. Alcoholic comas, hitchhiking, drug busts. The lady next to us says she lost an earring and Detox Woman just laughs. "Is that the worst thing you got? Hey, darlin', I have a brain aneurysm from shooting crushed glass in the vein of my neck because my biker boyfriend sold me tainted smack. I owe him five grand and he's still after me. His dealer wants him to finish the job, but he's too busy with the Harley and that's what saved my life. I put Drano in his gas tank. You get a biker worrying about his fuel line and he'll spend a lifetime fixin' it. God knows I loved that man. He used to beat me after I slept with his brother. You cain't never know what a man really wants."

Normal Guy is the guy who just sits there looking normal. Normal shirt, normal pants, normal shoes. When you speak to him it's "yes" or "no" answers. This guy has no luggage. He just gets on the bus and looks straight ahead. He has his hands on his lap. Right hand on his right knee. Left hand on the left knee. Fingers straight, as if he were sitting on a witness stand. You ask him where he's going and he's very vague. "To visit some people." This doesn't quite narrow it down. I feel like playing Twenty Questions, but he is so noncommittal I'm afraid I'll end up with, "I'm going to this town to see some people." The guy has no odor, no luggage, nothing to say. He never goes to the bathroom. He doesn't complain. When the driver stops to give us a 10 minute break, he calmly walks off the bus and stands in one spot for 10 minutes, then gets back on the bus, looking straight ahead, both hands on his knees. He wouldn't look out the window if there were a car wreck and a severed arm in the road. You could be like, "Hey! Is that an arm in the road?" No response. If the bus caught fire, he probably wouldn't get off until the bus driver said it was OK. He doesn't move, not even if we hit a bump. His body stays rigid. He's the Normal Guy. No luggage. Going to visit some people.

No Greyhound terminal would be complete without the video arcade. At the bus station, the only games available are the most violent: Mortal Kombat, Killer Instinct, Gunforce, Area 51, Total Fury. They are all somewhat self-explanatory. In these games, the object is to shoot, kill, punch and chop the opponent up into pieces. When you walk into the terminal, the games are all you can hear between the boarding calls. It's nothing but electronic screaming, gunfire, howling aliens, scraping swords, explosions and crunching bodies. Even when nobody is playing the games, this goes on 24 hours a day.

They say if you sit on the Entropy Car long enough, you'll develop a curved spine. These seats must be designed by blind midgets. Brainless laboratory test midgets with depressed motor skills. Every nerve in my back is pinched, and all I have is chump ibuprofen.

When I get up, I still feel like I'm sitting down. I might as well be sitting on a chair made of steak knives. Every position seems useless and I fidget around like a junky. I try to sleep and feel like Sisyphus pushing a goddamn rock up a hill, only to have it roll back down onto my nutsack. The guy who shot himself had the right idea. The only position you can sleep in is dead. I've got to remember to bring a gun next time I travel. I'll have to keep it well-hidden or everyone will want to use it. But before I take my own life, I want to kill the chimp who built this seat. I bet an electric chair is more comfy. What am I thinking? It's impossible. I'm hallucinating again. Maybe I can have a delusion of sleep. A clear waking-vision nap. Peaceful, calm, wide-eyed slumber. That's the state.

Why don't they have a snack bar and lounge on the bus like Amtrak? How much space can a wet bar take up? A couple seats? I could use a cold pint of pale ale and bag of chips right about now. I don't care if it's 10 bucks a beer. I'll pay for the convenience. This ride needs lubrication. Maybe they could build a tavern around the back three seats. Waitresses, cold Bud on tap, cool jukebox. What does juke mean? "Hey, bartender, what the hell kind of word is juke? Is that like jive, or short for junky? Get me a bar rag, I spilled some beer on my shirt. And a bag of pretzels. This is the way God intended human beings to travel. When did Greyhound start the lounge car? I need some quarters for the pay phone. Hey, who the hell played Mariah Carey? I'll take another pint of ale, please. Where's your bathroom? Over by the pool tables? Cool!" Must be hallucinating again.

When I get off to use the terminal dump station, every time it's the same thing, I accidentally walk into the women's bathroom and I don't realize it until I spot the hygiene box in the stall. There's something about riding this Giant Box of Sleepless Bodies that turns your brain to mashed yeast. In the stall next to me I can hear the frazzled-hair mom punching her child. She's smacking the kid and yelling, "Come on! The bus is leaving! Don't dilly-dally!" What a colossal bitch. The kid is not doing anything wrong. I want to say something. She's pulling his arm out of the socket. They're walking past me now and I feel like tripping her. "Oh! I'm so sorry. I must have some nervous tic in my foot. It's not supposed to jerk out straight like that." I could offer to help her up, then step on her hair and yank her arm. "Sorry again! I was just trying to help, and now this happens." Her own child would start laughing. "Mommy, that was funny. He stepped on your hair!" Some of the kids on the bus are well behaved. It's the parents who are circus freaks. The Bible says "Honor thy Father and thy Mother," but that was way before crack and *Wheel of Fortune.*

It's funny when old people have to sit in back. When we pick them up in a small town, they get on and look around, and all that's open is a couple of seats in the back. They get this worried look. An old lady in a fringed cowgirl shirt just got on. She's clutching her purse and shaking. Her gaze darts around like a distempered squirrel. Her eyes are bugging as she sits down right in the middle of the tattoo section. "These young men use coarse language. I need to get my Bufferin, but it's in my makeup case under the bus." Some guy passes her a bottle of red wine spiked with

Hydrocodone and tells her it's Ocean Spray Cranberry Drink. "Relax, Ms. Lansbury. You're gonna need more than Bufferin on this trip."

7

6:30 a.m., Dixon Paragon Bowling Alley Restaurant Lounge for breakfast. This town has got to be the suicide capital of the world. This horrible scab-infested diner is the most rotten food hole I have ever seen. It's like a prison cafeteria and every day is Halloween. I have no idea in the far pockets of my brain why this demon-seed driver stopped here. Something just doesn't feel right eating breakfast under a flickering Bud lamp. The waitress' name is Bev and she's got one foot in a convalescent home and the other in a 1950's Pall Mall cigarette commercial. The coffee is hot brown piss water. The driver is walking behind the counter like he's the manager. The only people who eat here are probably from Greyhound, because we're forced in like chunks of bad meat. Black people are trying to get served but they're being totally ignored and avoided like it's a Nazi Klan outpost with David Duke's twin alcoholic brother at the controls. It's now time to limp back on the bus, and I feel as if a set of Vise-Grip pliers were released from my nut sack.

The bus is almost empty, but some lady is singing out loud so I can't sleep. Nobody interesting to talk to. The people who do open their mouth just churn out inane babble on the weather in Flagstaff. When the bus is full, it's bizarre lawlessness. Passengers become violent in overcrowded settings—high-pitched arguments, broken life stories, sobbing dogmatic sermons on the Virgin Birth. But this ride is pure nothing. Rolling confinement and empty stares. I may have to open the emergency window.

Across the street there's the ABC Adult Book Center with a 24-hour, triple-X video arcade. Every bus terminal is always located in the most seedy flesh-exploitation zone of almost every low-rent town or metropolis that caters to the sick, perverted, degenerate scum, sex-addicted, pathetic jackoffs—and, of course, all those who ride Greyhound. I saw all kinds of local people walk into this porn-o-graphic snake-oil factory. Men, women, dogs, homeless people, policemen, clergy, off-duty cops, men dressed as police, pregnant mothers, grandmothers, a Wal-Mart manager and two goat farmers. It must be the extended winter that brings out the beast in these people—a cabin sex-fever psychic bend in the mind. Maybe that's what happened to the Donner Party. They fucked like mad rabbits in the snow until the food ran out, then just started eating each other. That's got to be one spooky video. And I bet they sell that here at the ABC Adult Book Center, peddling skin to a frozen town gone wrong. Lust-driven crazies flogging their burning genitals in sub-zero weather. It's like a deserted Ice Station Zebra out here with bright New York Times Square neon halogen red floodlights in every window. North Sodom, on the corner of Gomorrah and Beat Master.

Amish lady is drooling out the corner of her mouth. She's bent into a ball of black cloth, dreaming of Satan and microwave ovens. Why do so many Amish ride the bus? Did they lose the farm to the tax man? Tractor sold, horse and buggy repossessed—time to wander the country in search of the Promised Land. Bartering needlepoint for hot dogs they smack their dead face on the table and slobber at the bus terminal.

The driver won't shut the hell up on the PA. I want to jam something in his mouth. I need duct tape and a tennis ball. He's rambling on and on with the most moronic drivel. He's repeating himself. Yes, I know it's a nice day outside for the third time. I can see out the window myself! I don't want to hear about your favorite movie or the baseball scores. He's babbling a complete memory purge. It's like a flood of useless information about his pointless life and his family tree and trees we pass with acorns and now it's the weather again, chocolate chip cookies, worms his cat had, the Civil War. SHUT THE FUCK UP! Yes, I saw the junkyard. I know those are wrecked cars. I don't want to hear about your punk-ass Le Baron, the broken taillight you smashed or the drunk driving sermon. This is not a talk show. We don't care. I can't think. He's like a word processor hooked up to a microphone at a demonstration on nothing.

The Unabomber Type is like a science fiction version of the Old Amish Man. He speaks in a strange mathematical language. I met one once who just got out of jail for computer fraud. They're a little nerdy and they never eat anything. He's a cross between a Work Release, the Amish Guy and the Talking Fat Nerd without the talking. If they do speak it's all cryptic calculus stuff. The Unabomber Type I met spoke in a controlled whisper about Waco, American history, Islam, terrorism, 9-11, implantable chips, computer hacking, government conspiracies, United Nations and the New World Order. It all came out in two seconds like a flood of binary code. This was late at night and nobody knew what he said but it was creepy to me because I knew this guy was on his way to pick up or drop off a package.

The Child with No Parents is going to Grandma's house because Mommy and Daddy slit each others throats in a double suicide. This kid is demon-possessed, running up and down the aisle with his transformer doll. I tell him the doll is really a girl and he smacks me in the head and jumps into the Old Black Sleeping Lady's lap. Someone should keep an eye on this kid because he's a walking missing child. The next stop we make he'll hop into a car looking for a lost puppy. "Sit on your uncle's lap and he'll buy you all the transformer dolls you'll ever need. Lie in the upside down pentagram drawn in blood and hold this candle. Don't tell the police man because he's here too and he lives next door to the Mayor. We know certain people and we'll send you on the bus again to another town to meet more old men in long black robes. We also own Greyhound and we can get all the little boys we want. Don't cry or we'll put the rats on you again."

Every terminal has the Security Guard with the Wooden Leg. The leg never bends at the knee. It just whips out straight, like a marching SS. Nobody dares to look at it. You have to stare directly in this man's eyes when he's talking to you. His expression is pure steel. Everything gets quiet when he strolls past. Even babies stop crying. The leg is the Long Arm of the Law. The Prosthetic Leg of the Law. The Peacekeeper Leg—intimidating, professional and silent. You never hear it touch the floor. It glides by like a swinging pendulum of fear. Never underestimate the security guard with the wooden leg. It might not even be made of wood. It could be made of some sort of high-density composite fiberglass. Bulletproof; stain retardant. I've seen him spill two-thousand-degree boiling hot Kentucky Fried Chicken gravy on that leg, and it just rolls off his pants onto the floor, like the pants themselves are made of Kevlar or steel-belted fabric. Once I saw a small child grab his leg. Time stood still. He looked down with a piercing glare and the mother of the boy screamed, "Get the hell away from that man's leg, Timmy! Oh, my God, please forgive us!"

This new driver is wearing a toupee that somehow doesn't quite follow the contour of his head. It's kind of funny. The fake hair gives the back of his head an artificial look, like a mannequin is driving the bus. His skin is so pasty he could pass as a dummy in a wax museum. I'm afraid to ask him a question; I might hear a recorded message. It's starting to get warm in here.

This could be a problem. I wonder if he's an actual-size wax Greyhound voodoo doll. We could all be cursed. Everyone could get a headache or burning sensation in the crotch. Spontaneous combustion, unexplained sores and blank zombie stares.

Our next break at a convenience store, the Wax Driver is checking out the porn magazines. He could be sex addicted. I'll have to keep an eye on him. The Dominance Stop in Garden City is not the kind of place to buy potato chips. All the candy bars are shaped like genitalia. You can only eat so many black licorice whips before you break down.

Some guy next to me has his shoes off, and it stinks like a dead raccoon dipped in battery acid. We're supposed to arrive in the next town at 1 a.m., so it shouldn't be too bad if I can stand the funk of Shoeless Joe and his non-stop sports talk in my ear.

There's a funeral home right across from this terminal, with a creepy neon sign like a restaurant casino. I don't think death and neon should go hand-in-hand. Have some respect. "Hey, everybody! Come see the dead guy at Summer's Funeral Home! We've got an indoor playground for the kids and blackjack tables for Mom and Dad. Drinks on the house for the immediate family and one free trip to the fully stocked salad bar. The Righteous Reverend Randy Rollins will be your host and emcee for the dance party after the wake. And don't miss Comedy Night every Thursday, where you'll see the finest comedians from across the country. This week it's Jimmy "JJ" Dy-No-Mite Walker, as seen on *Good Times.* You'll laugh, you'll cry, you'll say goodbye to your lost loved one as he shuffles off this mortal coil. That's Thursday night. Don't miss the show! Also Friday, it's ashes-to-ashes non-stop techno-beat with D.J. Death Crazy D. Four dollars at the door. Goth Jam Friday Night!"

We stop in Salt Lake City, and two blocks up the street is the Mormon Tabernacle Compound. There's a giant wall, and the entire perimeter is surrounded by a 10 foot metal gate. All visitors are whisked through the side entrance and greeted by well-dressed Mormon security guards with black plastic Mormon nametags and walkie-talkie cell phones. They hustle us into the visitors' center and ask pointed questions. "Where are you from? What brings you here? What is your religious affiliation?" Dogmatic pamphlets are handed out, and we are told we can only go into the Tabernacle in small groups with a "guide." There are five large buildings inside these massive, castle-like walls. One building is obviously the Tabernacle; that's where the pre-teen boys sing. A smaller church to the left could be for outcasts. There's an intimidating, dome-like structure we're told nothing about. When questions are raised, the guides change the subject and direct our attention to the genealogy building, called the Hall of Records, where all the files on bloodlines are kept. The security guides are everywhere with those walkie-talkies. Neat, perfectly ironed white short-sleeved shirts and ties, close-cropped hair like Navy Seals. They're very cautious as they survey the crowd. The tourist group is broken up swiftly with machine-like precision by these smiling guides. I notice I've been separated from the crowd. Two guides approach me and began a quiet conversation on genealogy, bloodlines and my religious upbringing. Before I know what's happening, I have the Book of Mormon in my hands. When I try to give it back, they won't take it. It's like that sleazy sales technique where the salesman figures if you hold the object in your hand long enough, you'll be tricked into buying it. I all but jam it into the guide's stomach and he still won't take it. So I place it on the ground. The guides never look down; they just change the subject. Then a black custodian with white plastic gloves comes by and takes it away. He's the only black person I see there. And he's not wearing a Mormon nametag—just gray coveralls, a hairnet and surgical gloves. The whole thing happens so fast I get a sick feeling in my chest and the hair on the back of my neck stands up. I look at my watch. It's time to get back to the station. I mumble something about missing my bus and back away slowly. Their eyes never leave mine, unblinking, with that fundamental glare of *"You must have a lot of unanswered questions."* As I turn to run out the gate into the street I look back and they were already on the sidewalk. One guide snapping pictures in my direction and the other screaming into his walkie-talkie.

Back at the Salt Lake station there's a giant map of the United States on the wall, with all the Greyhound bus routes highlighted in purple like varicose veins. Directly above the map, there's a giant clock. The first thing that comes to mind is time and space and how much farther I have to go. The second thing that pops into my head is what kind of Jack Officer would put a map next to a clock at the bus station? When you're traveling cross-country on the Creeping Jesus Turtle Boat you don't need to be reminded of time and distance. As I gaze dumbfounded at this abortion of justice, I realize the fucking clock has stopped. And I just set my watch to this! My God, I've arrived at the flaming pit at the end of time. I'm face-to-face with eternity in the middle of Utah.

8

We're told to take everything off the bus. We load it all on a Powder River Coach. Powder River must be some kind of sub-contractor, because we're told Greyhound had run out of buses to Cheyenne. It seems cool at first, because it's a brand new coach with six video monitors hanging from the luggage rack. We depart at about 10:30 p.m. The new driver puts in a movie and I'm thinking, right on! This is the way Greyhound should run things. Movies, comfortable seats, no smell, the video's coming on, and I'm thinking maybe everything is going to be all right. Then the credits pop up: *"Man from Snowy River."* HOLY JESUS! And there are no headphones, so everybody on the bus has to listen to this stupid shit Western with Kirk Douglas all night long. I'm trying to sleep with the sound of hoof beats, gun shots, idiot dialogue. I can't read and I can't think. It's just *Man from Snowy River* blasting all the way to Nazi-fuck Cheyenne. Then, get this—the shithead driver locks us all on the bus for half an hour and just walks away. I can see other people in the terminal buying hot coffee, food, water. We're banging on the windows, trying to find the door lock. Some girl actually walked to the front of the bus and started honking the bus horn. It's frightening. We're trapped like rats. The Greyhound passengers are laughing at us, smoking cigarettes, chomping down on hot sandwiches. Finally, the driver comes back on and all he says is, "Does anyone have any questions?" There's a long, uncomfortable silence. So I raise my hand and ask the most obvious, "Uh yeah... Why were we locked on the bus for half an hour, you fucking deranged lunatic!" There's another long pause, then, "Come with me." The driver takes me off for this military hazing speech about controlled chaos and enemy combatants. I told him I bought a Greyhound ticket, not Powder River. AND I hate the movie *Man from Snowy River*. What is this? And why does everything end with the word *River* out here? Can I at least make a phone call? He smiles and says in the most evil good-old-boy accent, "Y'all free to make a call soldier." I get to the phone to call my parents, but I'm thinking maybe I should talk to an attorney, because I don't know what this is or where they're taking us. But there's no time, as our cage-with-wheels starts to pull out and I run back, pounding on the door. All my crap is in there, so I can't just say fuck this and stay in Cheyenne. He lets me on and he's laughing. Everybody is quiet and afraid. I climb back into my seat. The movie's still blasting away. Incredible. Un-fucking-believable.

We're out in the middle of nowhere. This town must have been built by Louis L'Amour in collaboration with Wes Craven on a bad day in a fevered dream. You have to watch your back in these here parts. Aggravated sodomy is just a practical joke. The Satanic sound of banjo music is in the air, pumping out of the jukebox at the Rabid Gopher Saloon. When the bus pulls into town, the collective literacy is increased by the power of 10. We are like gods to these people. One of the few places bus passengers can feel superior. The locals stare at our teeth in awe. When a black passenger steps off the bus, the children flock around him and reach out to touch his skin. The sheriff pulls up and watches from a distance with one hand on his six-shooter. Our driver greets him with a gift of Wonder Bread and peanut butter. He smiles and seems to relax. There are no street lights. As the sun goes down, people board the bus for safety. Sick dogs and old women surround us, begging for scraps of food. A deputy pulls up, and I notice a blood-soaked rope trailing behind his police cruiser. He steps out of the car and grabs a late straggler; she's trying to light a cigarette. Our driver runs over, and there's some kind of negotiation. More peanut butter is exchanged. They let her go and the driver hustles her on and shuts the door. We back out slowly as people gather around the bus with sticks. Rocks are being thrown, and the clang is like a hail storm. The driver jams on the gas and we're all pushed back into our seats. We duck onto the floor. Dust is flying, and I hear the sound of a barbed-wire fence being dragged along. There's a giant crunch and an airborne bounce. We must be going straight through a field. Dogs are barking, chickens are flapping. The dust settles and the ride smoothes out. I think we're back on the highway, but I don't look up.

Dark clouds up ahead. Tornadoes a half-mile wide are commonplace out here. Baseball-sized hail can beat a full-grown bull dead into the ground. The locals are jittery and timid. The driver comes on the PA and warns the mothers to keep their children away from the windows. Lightning can shatter tempered safety glass like cheap plastic. High winds can blow a bus around the highway like an aluminum can. A quick flash of crooked light appears in the sky with the sound of God's hammer and the passengers are now wide awake. We watch as an unmarked van loaded with electronic equipment and a satellite dish speeds past—must be tornado trackers. There are no warning sirens out here, so the driver switches on The Weather Channel. The signal is full of white noise, but we still plow through the storm. Another crack of lightning, a woman screams and her baby starts to cry. This driver has a death wish and he's not afraid to take us with him. The schedule must be maintained, so we hydroplane into the night. Out of nowhere, some guy up front starts talking out loud about the apocalypse: Bank closings, nuclear terrorists, famine, volcanoes, magma flow, meteorites striking the earth as it spins off course. I want to tell this guy to shut the hell up with the doom and gloom monologue. Hey, Mr. Koresh, you're scaring the children! Cut with the Revelation sermon! Flip back to the Song of Solomon or the Sermon on the Mount. Anything! It's hard enough on this devil boat. We don't need fear heaped upon fear with your Fire and Brimstone speech! Do I have to firebomb your seat?

At least they switched off the Kirk Douglas movie so we could get some sleep. The Powder River seats are softer than Greyhound's, so I doze off quickly—only to be awakened by the sweet sounds of country music. Actually, I find it easy to wake up to country music because of the adrenaline rush of anger: *"Oh, what the fuck is that? Ricky Skaggs? Ahhhh!"* I'm now wide awake. At least it wasn't the Little *River* Band; I would have died in my sleep. So we get dumped off at Hardee's for an hour and a half layover. More country music piped in on the Muzak. I'm sure we'll be picked up by another Powder River bus and get treated to the next John Wayne or Clint Eastwood movie. I need shooting-range ear protection. Maybe I can find some at the Trucker Oasis next door. They sell all kinds of crap; fluorescent orange camouflage hunting hats, shotgun shells, ephedrine Mini Thins and beef jerky. It's all impulse stuff right beside the cash register. George Jones tapes, pork skins, chewing tobacco, naked lady mud flaps, mosquito netting, *Thrifty Nickel*, duck calls, *Rules of Engagement* Waco video, fishing lures, live bait, Harley Davidson chain wallets, mint flavored toothpicks, lottery tickets, chigger bite repellent, and the *American Taxidermist* magazine.

Another Powder River bus pulls up to Hardee's and dumps the next full load of sleepless passengers. The place is crammed with tired bus people and locals. Every vehicle in the parking lot is a truck. No mini vans, no cars, no motorcycles. Nothing but goddamn trucks, feed caps and cell phones. These are serious ranchers. Hoss and the whole Ponderosa crew are here as we scatter to give them elbow room. These people carry guns. They own big tracts of land. They have gas pumps behind their truck cabs. Wyoming is Big Sky country and the sun is just coming up. The locals are leaving now in a feed-cap exodus to tend cattle or spread fertilizer, all filled up on Jimmy Dean pork sausage. We're burning daylight so they shove us out of the way without looking. I have yet to see any police or sign of a civil servant here. There's a big anti-government vibe in the air.

Next depot no one to pick up, nobody in town at all except a diseased frog hibernating below a dried-up pond. This must be the Grapes of Wrath stop where some member of the Joad family climbed off to reproduce with a goat. The water-head child grows up to build this gas station and shoots himself between the horns. The Man from Snowy River rides in to bury the corpse and board the place up before heading back to Denver to sell beaver pelts.

This is weird I'm back on Greyhound and our new driver is the same guy who locked us on the Powder River bus. He must work for both companies. Luckily we didn't get forcibly detained again, but his attitude hasn't changed. It's just more of that military terminology during his PA briefing—words like *vehicle, body count, controlled chaos,* no smoking in the *latrine*. If he finds any alcohol it's *search and destroy.* He's Colonel Kurtz from *Apocalypse Now!* I wonder if he torched grass huts in My Lai? I hope he doesn't recognize me from the bus lock-down. I could get singled out, ordered to scrub the floor with a toothbrush, do push-ups in the aisle, run in place. I hope we don't have this driver for too long, because we're going in circles. I feel like a rat in a cage on a wheel inside a maze with a fake piece of cheese at the end. I've got 20 blank pages left in this diary. When I'm done I'll probably chuck it out the window. Some hitchhiker will read one page and thank God he's standing on the side of the highway in the rain.

Holy fuck! A guy just attacked the driver while we were on the highway going 70 miles an hour! Somehow, the driver gets the bus pulled over as he's being punched in the head. I'm watching a bare-knuckle fistfight in the front of the coach! This is just too weird and confusing. Here's what happened. Out of the blue, this homeless-looking guy in a camouflage jacket gets up, walks to the front, and asks the driver to let him off on the side of the road. The driver says, "I'm sorry, sir, I can't let you off on the side of the highway. It's against corporate policy." So Homeless Camo Guy grabs the driver's hair and starts pounding on his head! The driver snaps like a rubber band. He's screaming at the top of his lungs: "You just put 47 peoples' lives in danger! That's attempted murder! And now we're going to be late!" Everyone is looking at each other, thinking, "So what? The bus is always late. We've been on this bus four days and it's never been on time." After things cool down, we wait for the police. Ché Guevara takes the seat behind me and I give him the revolutionary raised fist. I may not condone the violent overthrow of the Greyhound power cabal, but you can't blame the guy. First off, the driver is a complete asshole, he locked us all on the bus, was a total dick to every passenger and most importantly, the bathroom was almost unbearable at the time. This man was merely fighting for his basic right to get off the goddamn bus when he felt threatened or repulsed. We all felt his anger, but nobody thought it would go down like this. Personally, I would've waited until we made it to a terminal. I almost attacked the idiot driver who got lost twice. Maybe this full surprise attack was needed to send a message. A couple smacks to the side of the head and the driver is fully awake.

The State Troopers don't fuck around. The accused man is dragged off, handcuffed and tossed into the squad car like a common loser. Now the police want everyone on the bus to give up their *name, rank and serial number* with a written eyewitness account of what happened. They pass out a sheet of yellow notebook paper to each passenger. This takes an hour and a half so I make stuff up. I write a story about how the driver started punching him for no reason when he went up front to help a blind girl study the Bible.

9

I spot a fat Rush Limbaugh wannabe at the ticket counter with a Masonic pinky ring. He smiles as he picks up his cheap luggage and a plastic bag of clothes. There's a theory that the Freemasons control everything in a worldwide conspiracy. But with all his crap in a plastic bag, nothing seems to make sense. Bus station? World conspiracy? Plastic bag of socks? Maybe he's traveling the country free with a secret handshake. He walks to the counter, flashing complicated hand signals at the ticket rep. She doesn't seem to be responding so he raises both hands in the air, each arm forming a weird 90 degree angle and says, "O Lord, my God, is there no help for the Widow's Son?" Out of nowhere a driver comes by and whispers, "Tubalcain, my Brother, is the name of this grip." Very creepy.

What's in the bag? He keeps it close to his chest when he walks away, looking directly at me again. Am I being paranoid? I watch him at the phone later and he's punching numbers in like a typewriter. Must be some secret code message to a Scottish Rite Lodge. No talking, just a long series of numbers, *lots of sixes*. He keeps looking over his shoulder. I know he's got something in the bag. I notice the ring again. It's a shiny compass and square of the Great Architect.

An occult brotherhood obsessed with world domination infiltrating our national bus system? This would explain everything from the distorted PA to the blue piss water, and why we stop at every backwards poison-egg café from here to Dixon. It all seems to make sense. The banks, the Justice Department, the police, the school board, the Vatican, the ATF, CIA, NSA, FBI, MUFON, OPEC and now Greyhound, *all* infiltrated by the white man's Mafia. Decisions are made behind closed doors in smoke-filled chambers with strange handshakes and archaic rituals—on the wall a giant mural with the all-seeing eye of an insidious Greyhound looming above. The ancient Egyptians worshipped the dog-headed Anubis long ago, in the days when the sons of God slept with the daughters of men. And the word *bus* is taken from the word *Anubis*. Guard and protector of the deceased. The Egyptian Boat of a Million Years was actually a bus. The mythical bus of the afterlife for the Pharaoh's journey to the dark star Sirius. The Dog Star.

Still no sleep. I've got blurred vision, vertigo and a metallic taste in my mouth. Trees are spinning past like huge green mandalas. Night is coming on and semitrucks are passing by. Yosemite Sam mud flaps are mocking me. I'm somewhere in the back of the bus slipping in and out of consciousness.

There's a swastika in the tiles of the marbled floor! Someone should call Nuremberg and have this entire terminal burned to the ground. All of my worst fears have been realized. The Freemason who's been following me is laughing as I stare in horror at this symbol of evil. I want to scream: "There's a fucking swastika on the floor in permanent mortar! How clear does it have to be? Does anyone see this?" Am I being paranoid? Did the Nazis invent the bus like they invented the jet engine? When the trains were full, did they haul Jews on Greyhound to the Holocaust? I'm afraid to get back on. Are those smokestacks in the distance? Is this our last stop? Greyhound security comes by, tells me to move along and no more photographs please. He tries to take my camera, but I salute to the Fuhrer. He clicks his heels and smiles. I stumble away. I've got to protect this film. I'll hide it in my shoe. I'm beginning to feel nauseous. I run to the bathroom to throw up. There are swastikas everywhere. It's all too much. If I could only puke out my own brain and flush this scene down the toilet. More security personnel pound on the stall door and ask my destination. I snap to attention. "I want to lie in the sun with my white wife and offspring!" My God, what am I saying?

At the next station I spot a plaque of the Greyhound founder on the wall bearing this inscription: "Greyhound founder Carl Eric Wickman, a Swedish immigrant, turned a dream into a transcontinental transportation empire. At the age of 17, he emigrated from Sweden, leaving school in the 8th grade." A 17 year old who left school in the eighth grade?

Wickman's picture looked like an 8x10 promotional shot of Henry Lee Lucas, or a mean version of Harry Truman with a hundred atomic bombs to drop personally on whomever he pleased. As I stare at his forehead, my heart starts pounding and my eyes get itchy. This man is pure evil. He probably had a blood clot for a brain and a softened skull you could poke your finger in like a stick of hot butter. With little rodent eyes like two shiny black BBs that never blink, just gazing away into empty space. And a third eye on the side of his skull, dripping eye snot, a dead third eye just above his right ear like a milky-black protruding mole.

Excerpts from
Secrets of the Federal Transportation Reserve:
The Hidden History of Greyhound
By James Inman

Dark overlord Carl Eric Wickman, black magician, puppet master, trained by Aleister Crowley, raised by feral goats, brought together a group of financiers representing international bankers headquartered in Hibbing, Minnesota. Meeting secretly in November, 1910, for two weeks, during which time they drafted the Greyhound Act, later known as The Wickman Plan. After personally assassinating the Archduke Franz Ferdinand, Wickman was then able to launch the First World War. Simultaneously financing the Communist Revolution in Russia in 1917 and supporting Adolph Hitler's rise to power in Nazi Germany 1933. All this was accomplished with a network of employees forced into prostitution; which later became his personal bevy of mind-controlled drivers. The Greyhound workforce of today is the offspring of a Satanic plot to dominate the world, and Wickman's black-hearted desire to hypnotize and impregnate enslaved prostitutes.

Babies are crying like dueling banjos and I think I'm getting a brain hemorrhage. Every goddamn woman on this Cheap Ass Travel Dog has a fucking crying Eraserhead baby. Who are these women? Pumping out children and loading up the bus with diaper shit bags. I've never seen them breast feed, ever. Let the kid suck on something. You fuck every guy in town, you can't let your own child have one tit? Do something before I toss that thing out the emergency window. Change the diapers, shake it or chop off its head. I don't care. It'll probably keep crying out its neck. Next time I meet a pro-lifer I'm going to ask them if they ever rode Greyhound. They'll start working overtime at an abortion clinic after fifteen minutes of this. I'm reexamining the whole *save the women and children first* concept. Remember the final episode of MASH, when Hawkeye had to suffocate that baby in the back seat of a bus? It wasn't because they were in enemy territory. He choked the kid because it was bugging him. Maybe the guy who shot himself couldn't take the screaming babies. Give it up, Mommy. It's not like you're in a restaurant. Half the women in here have their banana tits hanging out anyway. Give that humanoid dwarf something to suck on. Or get some plastic stunt tits in here. I'll spring for the blow-up doll if you buy the half and half. A plastic doll never says no. I've never heard a kid cry so long. *I feel like crying!* It probably knows it's going to have to get a meaningless job and pay rent when it grows up. Maybe that's why babies cry. What a fucked-up world this is! And to think people made such a big deal about Saddam Hussein dumping babies out of incubators during the Gulf War. It really doesn't sound that evil right now.

I shove a quarter in the video game Area 51. A red plastic gun connected to a cable sends a signal to the screen exploding alien creatures. There's something about having a gun in my hand that makes me feel certain—Greyhound must be destroyed. This is a system fueled on greed, brutality, nepotism and slavery. A system so inherently evil, so mismanaged and inhuman, the passengers are pawns passed around the country into the convoluted outback of trailer homes and halfway houses, tossed aside or used as kindling for the fire of disease, boredom and the monotone of the endless highway of shame. A pointless trail with occasional stops for deluded coffee and corndogs filled with leftover scrap meat from the floor of an Iowa Beef death factory. Florescent Slim-Jims and the cold coffee of Satan. Rotary pretzels and Masonic hamburgers made from the flesh of weak passengers. A red toy pistol is my only release for this burning hatred. With an urge to destroy all that is wrong and broken, I imagine a spree killing. I rip the plastic .45 off its cable, run amok and provoke a violent standoff with the local authorities—shattered glass, mustard packets flying, children screaming, blood and dismemberment as I take this terminal down in flames.

10

This new driver's name is Elvis. That's his actual given name, and he's really laid-back. He gave us a rest stop for no reason. The bus is pristine and he has the temperature at an almost perfect comfort level. This is a good omen. The passengers are calm. Some look like they're asleep. Smooth ride. I'm sitting in the front row. Elvis is conversing about what it's like to operate a bus. He said one guy ran to the front of the bus while they were on the highway going 60 miles an hour. He grabbed the door release, jumped out, fell under the bus and was run over dead. He said one time a guy asked him for the fire extinguisher because a "fire" had broken out in the back, but the guy was hallucinating and had to be restrained. One lady took off her clothes and ran around a truck stop, naked and babbling. I asked about the suicide. He confirmed it. The guy shot himself in the chest in the back seat. Happens all the time, Elvis said. I should sit up front more often. You get the inside scoop.

It's 7:30 p.m. and we stop at Joker's Restaurant Lounge Casino. I ask Elvis if it was OK if I had a beer during our dinner break and he says, "I don't give a rat's ass. Just don't bring it on the bus." And he said it like he was annoyed at the stupid question. This is unimaginably cool, because every time we stop near a bar, all the drivers say if we try to buy beer we will be left on the side of the road. Finally, some freedom and respect. A man's got to have libation. Passengers are mingling; the bar is loud and rocking. Even the country music is not too repugnant. I'm tapping my foot and tipping the waitress. Maybe a bar fight will break out and I'll be forced to open a can of whoop-ass. I'm buying shots and flirting with the menopausal slot machine ladies. It's a good old shit-stomping time with cold Bud on tap and two dollar shots of tequila. Country karaoke, white-trash knick-knacks on the wall. The waitresses bend down, displaying a full-frontal cleavage shot with cheap perfume breeze every time the beer ran low. A giant smile floats across my face. This place was 45 minutes of heaven. Thank you, Elvis! I might need a motel. I can always catch the next bus in the morning. See'n how the wait staff is kinda friendly. I feel like a real truck driver, all hopped up on Quik Store speed. Grab me that Mixmaster microphone and I'll croon out a karaoke tune. I feel like Woody Guthrie now, all saddled up to the bar, but our time is up and the driver says we have to go. Sorry, ladies, I'd like to stay but the road keeps calling my name. A tight bus schedule waits for no man.

Acceptance must be the key on the long haul. Maybe the Amish truly have all the answers. They never proselytize. They teach by example. If you can tune in to their calm humility, you learn important life skills. Most people would go completely insane after a few smacks to the head with a suitcase, but the Zen-like patience of the Amish is a testament to the human spirit. I've seen crack-addled prisoners on work release set Amish beards on fire while they just nod and smile and offer their hat to burn as well. This is serene non-resistance. Violence begets violence. And zippers might not be necessary anyway. The code of the Amish is to feel compassion for all sentient beings great and small. I've seen the most deranged lunatics sit next to an old Amish man and slowly begin to lighten in the eyes and speak as politely as a gay Boy Scout. Almost everybody on the bus will mock the old Amish man, but when they see his head ablaze and not one tear in his eyes, we are all humbled and know he is truly a man of God.

If I were a bus driver, I'd stop whenever the hell I wanted. I'd let people smoke on the bus and drink tequila straight from the bottle. I'd jam on the brakes when anybody stood up. They'd flop around in the aisle and we'd all laugh and pour beer on their heads. I'd be on the PA the whole time, telling stories of my childhood, baseball scores, fake weather report. Drive on the median. Wear a balloon hat. Pass around a tank of nitrous oxide. I'd be the coolest driver. We'll take a tour through a cornfield and ram into a combine. Drop everyone off at their front door like a giant taxi. Let poor people ride free. I'd charge rich people double and kick them out in the worst part of Detroit. I'd keep their luggage and pass the clothes to the Bloodshit Lady.

I've been thinking. Things aren't as bad as they were when I first got on. I'm not saying this is the Love Boat, but right now I'm glad I'm not on a plane. Too much fear. I get claustrophobic. I feel that ominous thud when they close the door. It's just too spooky. I keep thinking about terrorists, hydraulic leaks and how the Nazis invented the jet engine. Everybody is too calm on a jet plane. What the airlines need is the Schizophrenic Tattoo Guy to stand up on every flight, screaming "We're all gonna die!" Just to keep the people in line. When you hear an airline pilot on the PA he's always like, "Don't worry, 'bout a thing. Cause every little thing's, gonna be alright." NO! I want a pilot who's on the edge of his seat. Not some goddamn no-problem Rastafarian. I don't think so, Capt. Marley. You are flying a fucking apartment complex through the air and I want to hear words like *check, re-check, I concur, roger* and *over and out*! Not that valium voiceover with the rock-a-bye-baby sing-song. I want a pilot with eight arms and five eyeballs, scanning and checking the cockpit like a space octopus on Methedrine! I feel ten times safer on a bus.

"SEVEN DIE WHEN BUS SMASHES INTO TRUCK"

I no longer feel safe. That headline appeared on the front page of a local newspaper at the last Quik Store. I pick it up and read: "The driver was Scott Wisner, 61, of Boothwyn, Pa., a 10-year Greyhound veteran who was making his last trip for the company. Also killed were Wisner's wife, age 34, and their 8-year-old adopted son."

Elvis is now in shock. I think we may get an extended break. I plan to stock up on food and wine. The no-alcohol policy has been dropped again. People are drinking and smoking. There's a quiet hush over the passengers. Normal Guy is weeping openly with his arm around Elvis. Even the prisoners are a little quiet. Sleepy Crackhead is talking to Stinky Priest about the meaning of life. This is all too much. Seven dead, one in critical condition, and seventeen injured.

The story also quoted Craig Lezenski, an executive officer for Greyhound: "This is one of the saddest days of my 22 years in the bus business. I want to express our sympathy to the passengers and our driver and their families."

When I ask Elvis if he knew Scott Wisner, he looks me dead in the eye, "Wisner was one of our best drivers. Always on time, like an old grandfather clock. He could do things I really cannot explain in words. We all looked up to him and tried to study his technique. I believe it's what the Taoist Masters called *wu-wei.* Doing by not doing, effortless, becoming one with the bus without judgments or pretense. I've seen him swerve to avoid turtles. That's how kind he was."

Greyhound flags are flying half-staff today, and for the rest of this week people will be stunned. This man, Wisner, was 61 years old with a wife of 34. He was probably preparing to take her on a cruise around the world after his retirement. His last run! How brutal. I hope this entire incident is investigated by the National Transportation and Safety Board. There's already talk of a conspiracy to silence this man because of his martyr-like compassion for the passengers. The people who knew Wisner said he never left anyone behind. He always tried to give five extra minutes at every stop and still somehow managed to keep to the rigorous corporate schedule. The conditions at headquarters are always severe business—bottom line. Drivers are pushed to unheard-of limits. "It's become like the Indianapolis 500 out there," Elvis mumbles, clutching the newspaper. "I don't know how much longer we can take it." I pass him the jug of wine and he takes a long hit. After half the bottle gets pulled out, he looks at me again. "Some heads are going to roll. He was probably up for a big pension. They snuffed him out with his entire family. I'm certain his brake lines were cut." When he passes the bottle back, it's almost gone. The break is about up, so Elvis barks out, "Let's roll, people!" We stumble on the bus and roll back onto the endless road. As we sit, all of us are wide-eyed and rigid, wondering what the hell is the point. A good man taken down with his young wife and child. It's all a pointless game, with human flesh grinding beneath the wheels.

11

Everyone is gone now. No Stinky Priest, no Detox Woman, no Talking Lady. I hate to say it, but I'm starting to miss everyone. The new driver has no personality. No PA briefing. He just gets on and drives. The bus is quiet with no smell. People come and go. Drivers come and go. I feel alone, with no one to make fun of. This diary is my only refuge, but now I can't even make stuff up. I should start talking to more people. Somebody must have a broken life story. Everyone looks so regular. Not unnaturally regular, like Normal Guy, just boring regular. No one looks at anybody. There are about four people and it's getting too quiet. Am I becoming one of the fucked-up people I write about? No one sits near me. I probably smell. I haven't shaved in five days. Maybe I'll be the next guy to snap. The driver will pull over and call the police. Someone will find this diary and understand it all. This will be the only clue to my condition. I'll try to kill myself out in the middle of West Memphis, babbling gibberish about work-release prisoners, looking for the driver who got lost. Where is he now? I miss the people I hate. Just like that book by Camus. The passengers are the dogs I beat, and when they run away I'm alone with no dog to torment but myself. Have I become the dog?

A black wave of depression sets in. I jump on the next bus and sleep for almost six hours. I arrive in Sacramento with a four-hour layover. So I walk to the liquor store down the street and buy a bottle of wine. I decide to wander around and try to strike up a conversation with a homeless guy. I find a 50-year-old, full-blooded Native American. We're passing the bottle and he's telling me stories about the '60s, San Francisco and LSD. I show him the crumpled news clipping on Scott Wisner. This leads to a discussion on death, religion, philosophy, homelessness, Native American history, Sitting Bull, Vietnam and social entropy. When the bottle is about empty, he wobbles off. Very cool guy. Drunken intellectual freak. I go back to the station and pass out in a TV chair, which is no big deal because everybody sleeps 'till the bus comes along. Sacramento is worse than Omaha. Complete wasteland of degenerate scum, and I'm just part of the woodwork. I doze off for a while and the barking sound of the PA comes on: "Bus 153 to Portland now boarding. Wake up, you loser shitheads. Thank you for riding Greyhound!"

I get up and wait in line, minding my own business. I hand the guy my ticket. The fascist punk baggage handler takes one look at me and says, "I'm sorry sir, I can't let you on because you've been drinking. Your breath smells like alcohol." I'm like, "And? So what? The bus smells like a heated turd. I had a couple beers across the street to even things out." He says, "I can't let you on the bus. It's against Greyhound policy." So I said what any drunken idiot would say: "You killed Scott Wisner!" This was not what I meant to say. I wanted to say, "No problem. I'll wait for the next bus. I sincerely apologize. You're a good worker." somehow it didn't come out right. He calls security, and I am now physically removed from the Sacramento Greyhound station. Twenty bucks in my pocket. Drunk like a retarded sea turtle. So what do I do? I can't go back in and act like nothing happened after the security guard tried to mace me. I'm too tired to find the highway and hitchhike. All the motels were over a hundred bucks a night. I have no friends in town to sleep on a couch. Better get a 40-ounce and think this over.

I go to the liquor store and pick up two bottles of Colt 45, set them on the counter and pull out my wallet. The booze pimp says: "Sorry, sir, we can't sell to homeless people." I'm like: "What? You rotten punk! I'm not homeless! I just got kicked out of the bus station!" He says: "We have a homeless problem here, and we reserve the right to refuse service. So move along or I'll call the police!" What is this, some kind of Kafka mind grip? I start screaming. "You fucking Freemason! Is this is part of the plan?" Not good. He grabs his cell phone and starts dialing. So I stumble off into the street, and that's when I notice the entire street is filled with homeless people. They're all over the place, pushing shopping carts, pissing in the street, sleeping on the sidewalk. Now I'm on a mission. The line has been drawn. I'll redistribute wealth evenly among the poor. I'll organize a beer run and we'll drink until dawn. I find a guy who looks respectable, give him 20 dollars to go into the store for me, "Bring back enough alcohol to lay waste to this street." He takes the money; tip toes in, and buys a wine cooler as I watch him through the window. He comes out and just takes off running. "Incredible! You fuck! I'm fucked! I trusted you with my last twenty, you crack freak!" I'm too drunk to catch him, so I sit on the curb next to this black homeless kid about sixteen years old. He's laughing. I'm laughing. We start talking for a while and I show him the diary.

It's getting dark and I ask him where he sleeps. He said he's got a place in the park. He takes me to this deserted playground. There's no grass, just dirt. I crawl up in the fetal position on dirt clods and rocks. I wake up in the middle of the night. By this time, I sober up and realize I have to be in Portland by tomorrow. So I swallow my pride, call my friend Emery and he wires some money. I take a taxi to the airport and walk onto the plane, covered with dirt from head to toe, smelling like an open beer keg. Nobody says a word. I sit down. We take off. The flight attendant comes by and asks if I would like something to drink.

ABOUT THE AUTHOR

James Inman is an award winning comedian living in Kansas City. He has performed at the prestigious Edinburgh Fringe Festival, the Montreal Just for Laughs Festival and is the 1997 winner of the San Francisco Comedy Competition. James divides his time between used book stores, a computer and the occasional retreat to a psychiatric hospital.

Printed in Great Britain
by Amazon

46079742R00050